THE
SPACE RACE

© Aladdin Books Ltd 1986

First published in the United States in 1987 by Gloucester Press
387 Park Avenue South
New York NY 10016

ISBN 0-531-17041-1

Designed and produced by Aladdin Books Ltd
70 Old Compton Street
London W1

Library of Congress Catalog Card Number: 86-82689

Printed in Belgium

The front cover photograph is a montage of the Challenger and astronaut Bruce McCandless wearing a jet pack – the Manned Maneuvering Unit – on his back. McCandless was the first astronaut to leave his spacecraft without a lifeline. The back cover photograph shows a model of the spaceplane Hotol.

The author, Pearce Wright, is science editor for The Times, London.

Dr. David Baker, the consultant, is the director of a space consultancy company. Dr. Baker was a consultant with NASA for twelve years, and a consultant to the American space program for a further six years.

Contents

THE
SPACE RACE

PEARCE WRIGHT

Illustrated by
Ron Hayward Associates

Gloucester Press
New York : Toronto : 1987

Introduction

On January 28, 1986, the American space shuttle Challenger exploded, killing its crew of seven. This disaster was followed by the failure of two unmanned rockets carrying major satellites. The powerful American space industry was thrown into a crisis of confidence. The international space race entered a new phase.

The competition to use and control space is what the space race is about. Rivalry in space is largely a struggle between the two superpowers, the United States and the Soviet Union, but there are also many other contestants in the race.

Why is the control of space so important? (Space technology is concerned with military developments such as satellites for surveillance and spying or the monitoring of nuclear weapons tests.) Countries also want a share of an expanding market for launching commercial and scientific spacecraft for international telephone and television links, weather forecasting and scientific research. As a result, the motives for joining in the space race are a mixture of military security, profit and national pride. This book is about how the race began, what it involves and where it is going.

▷ The photograph shows the destruction of the Titan 3 booster, carrying a "Big Bird" spy satellite. Coming so closely on the heels of the Challenger accident, this effectively grounded the US space program. Titan was the United States' most powerful unmanned launch vehicle.

The race to the Moon

These photographs show history being made by the crew of Apollo 11, Neil Armstrong, Edwin Aldrin and Michael Collins. As Armstrong put his left boot on the lunar surface, an estimated 600 million television viewers around the world could just distinguish the words, "That's one small step for man; one giant leap for mankind."

On July 20, 1969, the United States landed a man on the Moon. This achievement, which may rank as the greatest of the 20th century, cost the United States a staggering $24 billion.

President John F. Kennedy began the space race in 1961, when he promised the American people, "We will put a man on the Moon by the end of the decade." It was an ambition intended to boost national pride and to demonstrate to the Soviet Union the superiority of American technology. Behind it there was also a lingering resentment that it was the Russians who had begun space exploration with the first satellite, Sputnik 1, in 1957.

Nine weeks after the American Moon landings, the Russians made an unmanned landing on the Moon with Luna 16. The race had not only been won by the United States, it also revealed different attitudes between the superpowers concerning manned and unmanned space technology.

Conquering space today

Space has been called the last frontier. Flights by astronauts have been compared with the exploits of the great navigators like Christopher Columbus. In today's context, space is the ocean.

Whereas the reasons behind the race to the Moon were based on national pride, the reasons behind the current space race are more complex. Whoever conquers space today gains power and is the forerunner in many ways: in the field of communications, in military matters and in spying and surveillance. As far as high technology industries are concerned, countries that stay out of the race may face a bleak future.

Only the United States and the Soviet Union can put men into space. But there are many countries who now have large unmanned rockets that can launch spacecraft. The new rivals include Japan, China, India and the European Space Agency (ESA) – a group of ten European countries and Canada.

▽ An increasing number of countries are launching vehicles into space. This is adding to the problem of space debris. In order to avoid collisions and to make sure discarded rocket casings and other pieces are not mistaken for incoming missiles, the United States Air Force monitors all objects in space from 4cm (1½ in) in diameter. The work is part of the North American Air Defense system (Norad).

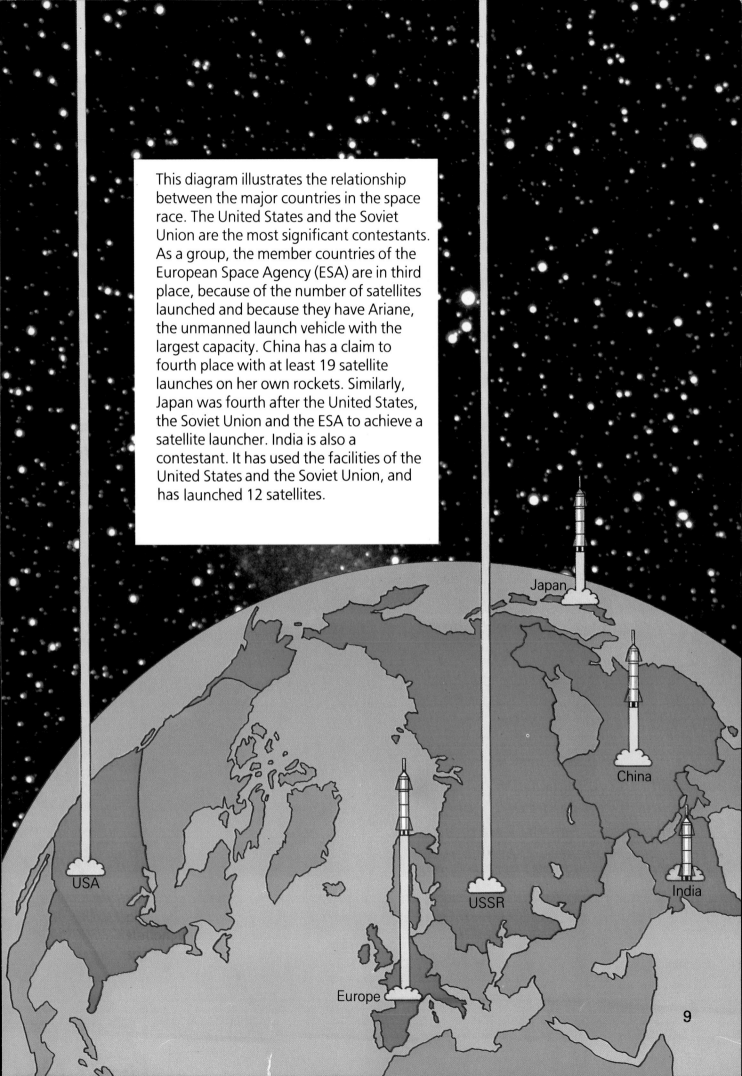

This diagram illustrates the relationship between the major countries in the space race. The United States and the Soviet Union are the most significant contestants. As a group, the member countries of the European Space Agency (ESA) are in third place, because of the number of satellites launched and because they have Ariane, the unmanned launch vehicle with the largest capacity. China has a claim to fourth place with at least 19 satellite launches on her own rockets. Similarly, Japan was fourth after the United States, the Soviet Union and the ESA to achieve a satellite launcher. India is also a contestant. It has used the facilities of the United States and the Soviet Union, and has launched 12 satellites.

Japan

China

India

USA

USSR

Europe

9

The US program

The reusable space shuttle, the Orbiter, is the star of the US space program. Until the Challenger disaster, a fleet of four shuttle Orbiters, the part which looks like an airliner, had completed 24 missions. They had carried 91 astronauts into space, launched 24 commercial satellites and conducted countless scientific experiments.

The astronauts of NASA (the National Aeronautics and Space Administration) showed it was possible to recapture satellites. Two were repaired and put back in orbit. Two others were brought back to Earth for maintenance. Also for the first time, apparatus for complex scientific research was returned to the ground for examination. This included the return of a complete laboratory called Spacelab.

Behind the scenes, however, the successes were overshadowed by the high costs of each mission. They were costing an average of $150 million a mission. Customers, such as TV companies, were being charged $15 million, which was intended to repay development costs.

△ The largest of the millions of components which make up the shuttle is the huge External Tank, on which the Orbiter, housing the crew, is perched like a resting butterfly. Since the tank contains about 800 tons of liquid oxygen and liquid hydrogen to fuel the rocket engines, the complete spacecraft is a potential flying bomb. When the shuttle exploded in 1986, an escape was not possible.

△ The ability of men to work in space is important for military and scientific purposes. In shuttle flights before the Challenger disaster, astronauts worked in the Orbiters' cargo holds to retrieve and repair damaged satellites.
Plans to go ahead with an $8 billion permanent American space station have now been modified to include less work by astronauts and more by robots.

The Russian program

By 1986, Russian cosmonauts had spent about 2,000 days in space compared with 480 days by American astronauts. The longest Russian stay, 237 days, would be enough time for a manned spacecraft to travel to the planet Mars!

Because of the long duration of flights, the record book has an impressive list of Russian firsts. The first space walk and the first link-up of two vehicles and transfer of crews between them are among them. The Russians were also the first to prepare a manned space station, Salyut. Manned spaceflight actually began with the Russians, with Yuri Gagarin's one-orbit journey in Vostok 1 in 1961.

◁ Valentina Tereshkova, pictured outside a Salyut space station, was the first woman in space in 1963 in Vostok 6.

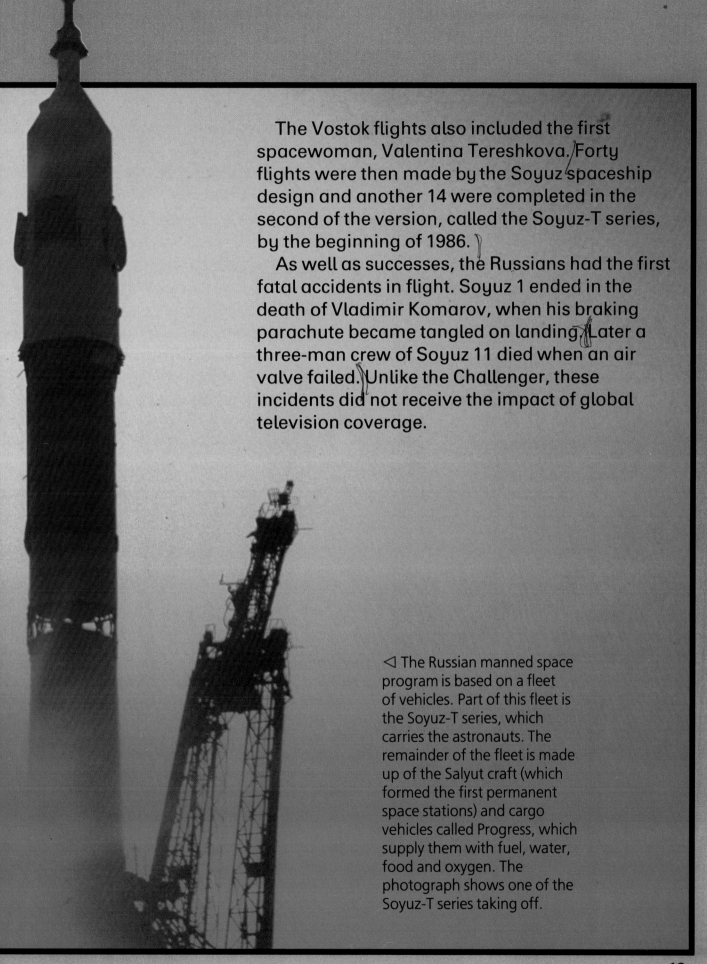

The Vostok flights also included the first spacewoman, Valentina Tereshkova. Forty flights were then made by the Soyuz spaceship design and another 14 were completed in the second of the version, called the Soyuz-T series, by the beginning of 1986.

As well as successes, the Russians had the first fatal accidents in flight. Soyuz 1 ended in the death of Vladimir Komarov, when his braking parachute became tangled on landing. Later a three-man crew of Soyuz 11 died when an air valve failed. Unlike the Challenger, these incidents did not receive the impact of global television coverage.

◁ The Russian manned space program is based on a fleet of vehicles. Part of this fleet is the Soyuz-T series, which carries the astronauts. The remainder of the fleet is made up of the Salyut craft (which formed the first permanent space stations) and cargo vehicles called Progress, which supply them with fuel, water, food and oxygen. The photograph shows one of the Soyuz-T series taking off.

European Space Agency

A third force has been at work in space technology for more than 20 years. It is the European Space Agency, a group composed of Belgium, Denmark, France, Germany, Italy, Netherlands, Spain, Sweden, Switzerland, U.K. and Canada. It is perhaps best known for the Ariane rocket, which launches commercial and scientific satellites. ESA's space agenda is ambitious. The idea is to establish European independence in most areas of space development, covering most types of satellites, launch vehicles, Earth observation and telecommunications operations. The program will lead to manned flights and manufacturing on space stations.

Europe is a leader in satellite design and manufacture. There is now an independent network of European weather, land survey and telecommunications spacecraft, most of which have been put in orbit by Ariane. Getting this far was as much a political as a technical achievement because the member countries have different ideas. In fact, the dominant partners – Britain, France and Germany – have strong conflicting views. However, since 1975 members have agreed to compulsory, optional and national projects.

esa

△ The *Giotto* spacecraft, launched by Ariane, flew past Halley's comet in 1986. It was a great achievement. It was also a sensational demonstration of 17 nations sharing in a project which none of them would have been prepared to pay for independently.

Some of the stresses and strains in ESA were further relieved almost by accident. The member countries became united in their disapproval of the US government when it tried to restrict the transfer of technology to Europe. The Americans did this partly for commercial reasons. But their main fear was that advanced technology would reach the Russians. ESA also ran into problems over the space laboratory, Spacelab, which it built for over $1 billion for flying in the US shuttle. ESA had hoped to get its investment back by selling four more Spacelabs to the United States. However, NASA only bought one.

DESTROYED F-27

DAMAGED MI-8/HIP

DESTROYED MI-8/HIP

Surveillance and spying

Surveillance and spying are two of the most important pressures behind the space race. Spy satellites like the KH 9 "Big Bird" satellite carry powerful camera equipment in a low orbit for a matter of months. Spy satellites were developed initially to detect missiles the moment they were launched. They are also used to watch for breaches of nuclear test ban agreements and to make detailed maps of military movements.

The Russians use men as spies in space more often than the United States. Cosmonauts aboard a space station in low orbit "observe" large areas and can transmit the information back, without the need to process film parachuted to the ground. American satellites, however, have advanced computer technology that can cover an enormous area and can actually *transmit* photographs.

Spy satellite photographs are not released to the public. The photograph on the right, taken by a commercial satellite, shows the site of the disaster at the Chernobyl nuclear power station (circled in white) in the USSR in May 1986. The photograph above (taken by a high-flying airplane) shows the damage done by US bombers to Libya in 1986. Spy satellites are better equipped to photograph events like these, as they can take much more detailed photographs. This is vital, particularly when a government is reluctant to supply information about an event that is important internationally, such as Chernobyl.

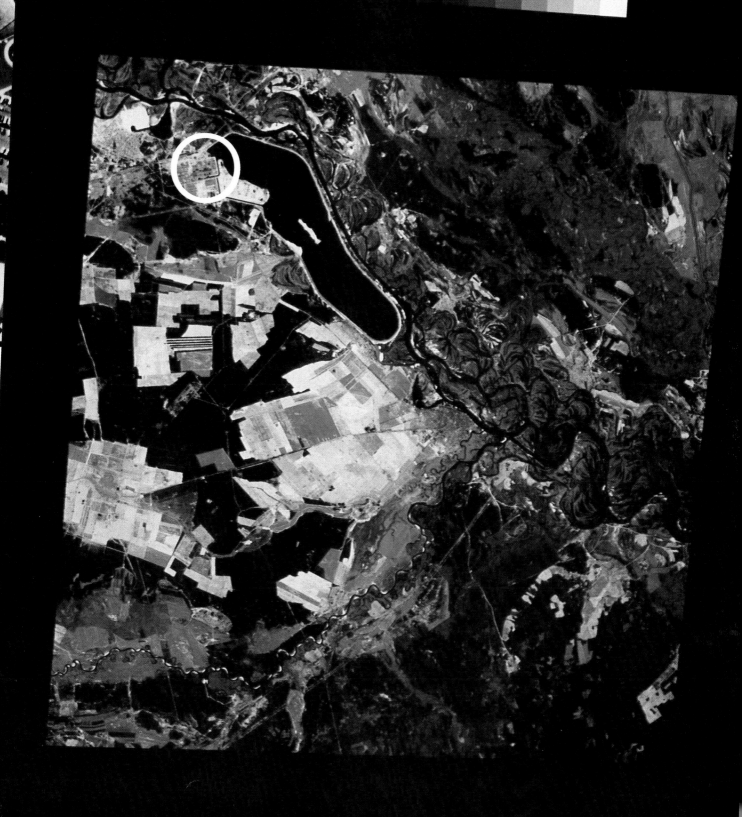

N 51°18'/E030°10' AZ:161°36' EL:53°54' OR:13°36'00" INCID:R3°   09H 11MN 01S Q: NIB

Military use of space

Military use of space is another great pressure behind the space race. In fact, the strongest driving force behind the Russian-American space race involves the fear that the other might achieve military dominance if it were the first to take control of space. There is a belief that the Strategic Defense Initiative ("Star Wars") system proposed by President Reagan is the first military use of space. That is certainly the impression given in Russian criticism of the idea. In practice, space technology grew out of the work on missiles by the US Air Force and Army, and by their counterparts in the Soviet Union.

There is a major difference between the superpowers which affects their military activities. In the US the amount and purpose of money to be used on space is examined publicly.

▽ The plan to put permanent space platforms carrying weapons in orbit, part of the "Star Wars" program, has met with a lot of criticism. There have been many protest demonstrations, an example of which is shown in the photograph. Senior scientists have also mounted campaigns against the scheme. In the United States, many have left laboratories which have accepted research contracts to develop the necessary techniques.

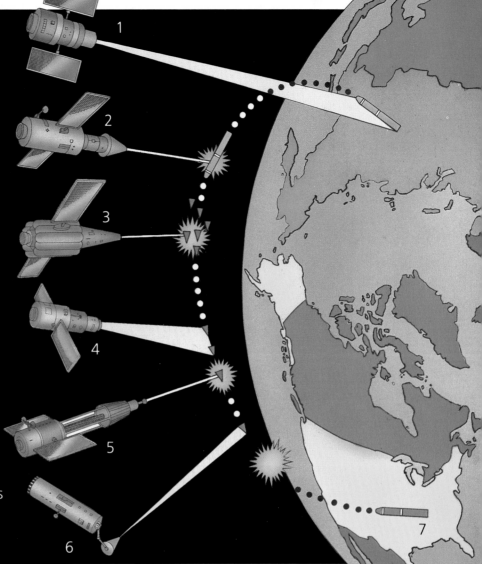

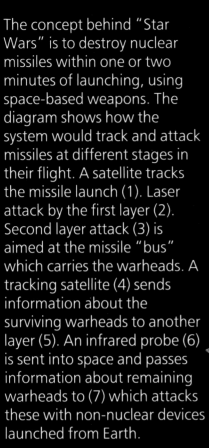

The concept behind "Star Wars" is to destroy nuclear missiles within one or two minutes of launching, using space-based weapons. The diagram shows how the system would track and attack missiles at different stages in their flight. A satellite tracks the missile launch (1). Laser attack by the first layer (2). Second layer attack (3) is aimed at the missile "bus" which carries the warheads. A tracking satellite (4) sends information about the surviving warheads to another layer (5). An infrared probe (6) is sent into space and passes information about remaining warheads to (7) which attacks these with non-nuclear devices launched from Earth.

Often less money is awarded for space than is wanted by the US Department of Defense. For example, in 1986 they were allocated $12 billion less than they asked for. This is not the case in the Soviet Union – the military is not publicly accountable for how much money it spends on space projects. As a result, the Russians have conducted many times more military launches than the Americans.

There is a United Nations treaty against the use of space for offensive purposes. But in 1976 this was broken when the Russians renewed tests of a small satellite that could be guided to another satellite in order to destroy it. The United States now wants to develop a similar anti-satellite system.

Commercial uses of space

Commercial reasons are a major force behind the space race. There is a growing market for the launching of commercial spacecraft to provide international telephone and television links and for weather forecasting.

Space exploration has changed our lives – television is an obvious example. Major news events, such as the Olympic Games, are available at the flick of a switch. Yet this only became possible 20 years ago. In 1965, a satellite was put into orbit by a group called Intelsat, to which 109 countries belong. Today, its communications satellites girdle the Earth. They are on duty twenty-four hours a day, educating, entertaining and helping people.

▽ Every corner of the world can be "seen" by weather satellites. The picture below is a weather map of the world showing global rainfall (blue) over the oceans.

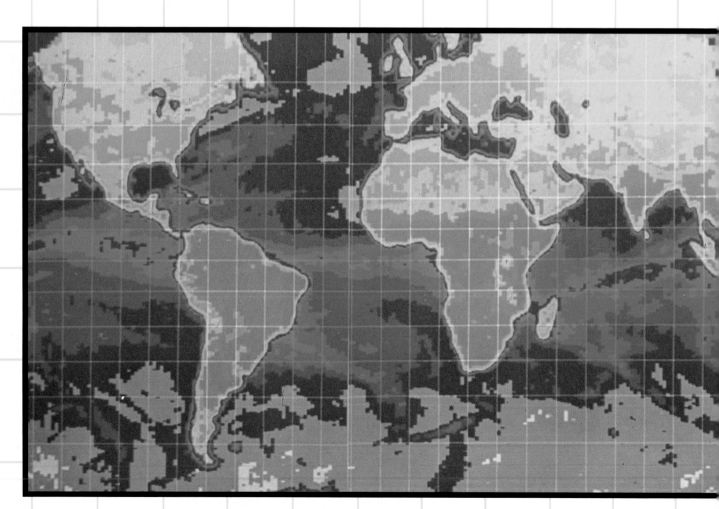

Satellite communications have made an enormous impact on areas which previously had no hope of radio or telephone reception. A dramatic example came in India in 1975. The new Indian Space Research Organization negotiated the loan of an American satellite. It was maneuvered over the Indian Ocean. Using receiving aerials, often made from chicken wire, more than 10,000 out of 520,000 villages took part in an experiment of receiving educational, health, agricultural and current affairs broadcasts on a communal television system. Following that success, a permanent Indian satellite extended TV coverage in 1985 from 20 per cent to 70 per cent of the population.

▽ The first communications satellites were like electronic hat boxes. But the famous Early Bird, or Intelsat 1, launched in April 1965, had one channel that could carry 240 telephone calls and one for a television circuit. The latest design of Intelsat spacecraft, shown in the photograph, has 15,000 channels.

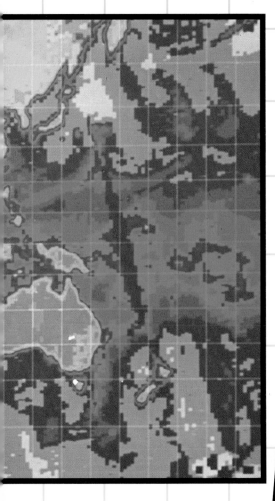

Disaster!

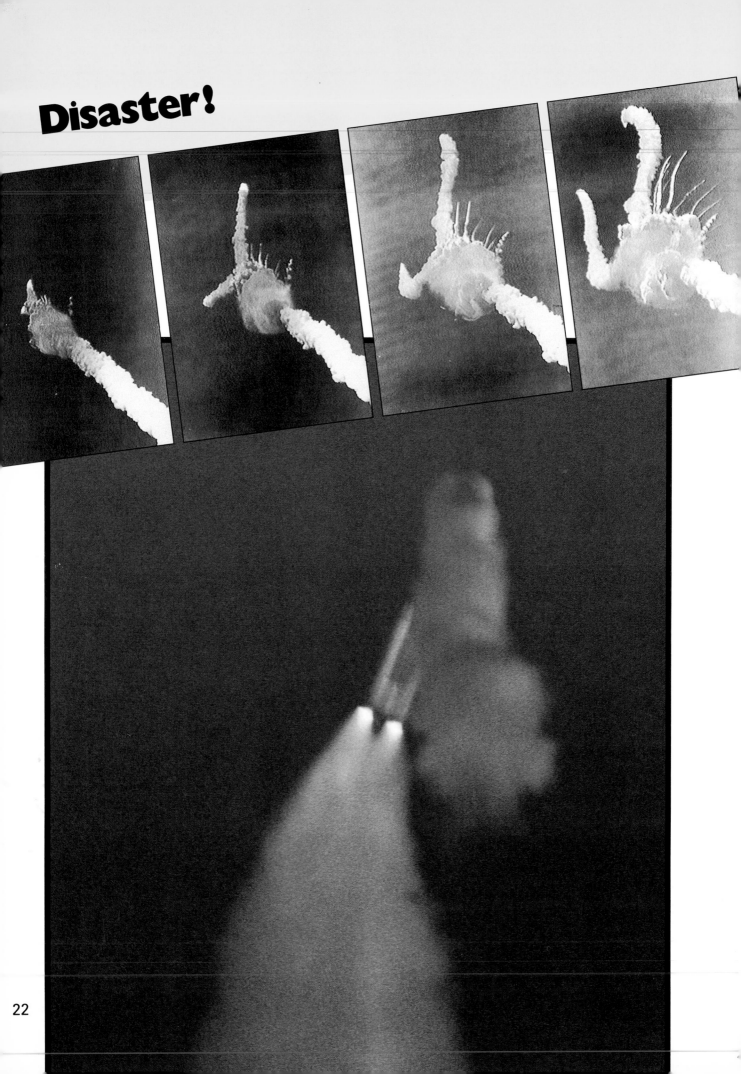

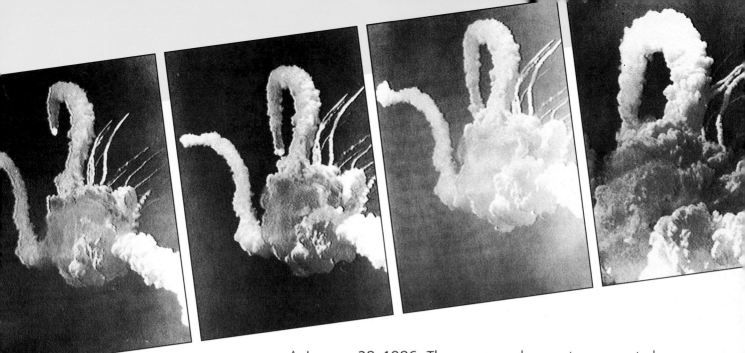

△ January 28, 1986: The space shuttle Challenger explodes. Having argued so well about the cost-effectiveness of this form of transport, NASA was under great pressure to keep to a schedule and a budget. A civilian teacher, Christa McAuliffe, was one of the victims of the disaster.

The failure of the Delta 178 on May 3, 1986 (shown left) was a great disappointment for the US space industry. When its motors failed to operate properly, the order was given to blow it up. Delta was used to launch unmanned satellites, and at the time of the explosion it was carrying the latest design of weather satellite. The accident was the third failure of the year in five US launching attempts. It was to have been one of the last Delta flights, as it was intended that the shuttle would take over launching most satellites.

Following the series of disasters in 1986 – and in particular the Challenger tragedy – fears were expressed that safety was being sacrificed in the race to control space. The Challenger disaster effectively brought the United States' vital intelligence, military, commercial and scientific missions to an abrupt halt, projected in 1986 to last for two years. How could it happen?

The precise cause of the explosion was a combination of bad design and bad management. A component failed because there was a leak of gases through an imperfect joint. The decision to launch was taken against expert engineering advice.

The seeds of the Challenger disaster were actually sown many years previously. NASA compromised and modified the design when the US government put a limit on the money available for the project. Pressure on management to stick to a budget, and more importantly, to a timetable had clouded judgment on safety.

A major rethink...

Every aspect of the world's space programs has come under scrutiny since the shuttle disaster. Many people argue that too much money is spent on the space race. However, if NASA's budgets for the past thirty years were added together, the figure would amount to less than one-third of the US annual budget for health, education and welfare. In fact, the US spends less on space projects each year than it spends on cleaning its National Parks. In return for that relatively small amount, the nation gains enormous commercial benefits from space.

The arguments about manned versus unmanned spacecraft have also resurfaced. Some scientists believe that everything done by astronauts could be achieved at one-tenth of the cost by using unmanned spacecraft. Yet many think that manned spaceflight is essential to our future in space.

▽ An artist's impression of the Russian shuttle. Its capacity, capable of placing 30 tons into low orbit, is the same as the United States' type. But the Orbiter itself is a heavier craft, and the booster rockets could be used as an unmanned "heavy lift vehicle" to put 100 tons into low orbit.

...next moves

Future developments in the space race include designs for many manned vehicles. The Russians are developing their own shuttle. According to scanty information, the Russian vehicle has an Orbiter-type spaceship riding on huge boosters. Similarly, France is determined to go ahead with ESA in the development of its manned shuttle, Hermes, which would be about half the size of the American version. In the United Kingdom, British Aerospace and Rolls-Royce are developing the first true spaceplane, Hotol (horizontal take-off and landing). The advantage of this technology is that it could be flown from a runway into orbit and back.

△ The pictures show a model of Hermes, left, and the British spaceplane Hotol, right. The French Hermes would be launched on top of Ariane 5, the booster planned for launch in 1997. The spaceplane Hotol combines the aerodynamics of supersonic jets like Concorde and the rocketry of the shuttle. Hotol can be automatic or piloted and would launch satellites cheaply.

The race widens

Seven months after the Challenger disaster, President Reagan announced that NASA could build a replacement shuttle, costing $2.8 billion. But the US government imposed some restrictions. In the future, the shuttle would be used only for military and scientific missions and not for any new commercial ventures.

This decision signaled a new turn in the global space race. It provided an opportunity to the other countries with launch vehicles who had been trying to develop their own space programs. A commercial satellite launch service was already on offer by ESA. China entered the market place with its Long March 3 booster, which could only carry a small payload but was relatively inexpensive. The Chinese planned to provide 12 launches a year for foreign customers.

▷ Japan showed its potential in space technology when it launched its H-1 rocket in 1986. But its chance of getting a share of the commercial market will rest on the next generation of boosters which will be made totally in Japan.

The Soviet Union stepped in with bargain-price launches costing $18-20 million – half of Europe's Ariane's cost. However, the American government forbids any satellites containing US components from going to the Soviet Union. The majority of satellites built in the West have some American components.

The fourth contender for launch services was Japan. The opportunity arrived a bit early for the Japanese National Space Development Agency, which had just launched the first of its H-1 series of rockets. They contain 20 per cent US technology, and the license for their use prevented them from being offered to foreign customers without American approval. But several countries began talks with the Japanese about an independent commercial service.

▷ China's first carrier rocket being launched in 1970. China can now launch small satellites quickly and at "bargain" prices.

Bridge between worlds

Although the short-term picture looks rather confused for NASA, the pressures behind the space race are as clear as ever. The motives of military security, national pride and profit will keep the momentum of the race going. If anything, the 1986 disasters have merely intensified the pressures.

NASA has drawn an optimistic picture for the long-term future. A group of US specialists has produced an ambitious report called "Pioneering the Space Frontier: Our Next Fifty Years." They predict human settlements on the Moon by 2017 and bases on Mars by 2027. They envisage a 21st-century "bridge between worlds." This would consist of a series of spaceports between a large space station in Earth orbit and permanent bases on the Moon and Mars. A heavy-lift cargo vehicle, like the Russian one, and a passenger spaceplane, like the British Hotol, would perhaps be needed. Other ideas include solar power satellites beaming energy to Earth and the mining of asteroids for minerals.

However fantastic all these proposals may seem, science fiction could soon become fact. Moreover, turning these ideas into reality may well become part of the space race of the future.

Mars, photograph left and below, is not an unknown planet. Visiting spacecraft have shown it to be more desolate and hostile than the worst desert on Earth. But recent space catastrophes have not dampened the enthusiasm of those countries that are determined to stay in the space race and one day reach Mars.

An early design of NASA's space station, planned for assembly in the mid-1990s.

Space facts

1957 Oct 4 Space exploration begins with Sputnik 1, launched by Russia. It carries two radio transmitters.

Nov 3 A dog called Laika, carried in Sputnik 2, shows animals can survive weightlessness.

1958 Jan 31 The US enters the race with Explorer 1. Its instruments reveal the existence of zones of radiation trapped in the Earth's magnetic field.

Oct 1 NASA officially forms to take over rival projects of the armed services and "achieve at the earliest practicable date, orbital flight and successful recovery of a manned satellite."

Dec 6 The opening shot at the Moon by the United States, with unmanned Pioneer 3, fails to reach it.

1959 Sept 14 A Russian probe, Luna 2, crashes about 400 km (250 miles) from the visible center of the Moon.

Oct 6 Pictures of the far side of the Moon are relayed from the Russian Luna 3.

1960 April 1 The forerunner of the American spy and surveillance satellites is launched in the form of TIROS, which transmits the first series of pictures of the Earth.

1961 Jan 31 The chimpanzee Ham is the first ape to be put in orbit, in the third flight of an American Mercury craft.

April 12 Manned spaceflight begins with Yuri Gagarin's flight of 1 hour 48 minutes in Vostok 1.

May 5 Alan Shepard follows for the United States in Freedom 7 in a flight lasting 15 minutes 22 seconds. He is weightless one-third of that time.

1962 April 27 A third country gets a stake in space technology. A scientific satellite, Ariel 1, built in Britain and launched by NASA, conducts radio and X-ray astronomy observations.

August 26 NASA launches Mariner 2 to obtain photographs and measurements of Venus.

1963 June 16 Valentina Tereshkova, aged 26, is the first woman in space in Vostok 6, completing 48 orbits in 70 hours 50 minutes.

1964 July 28 Ranger 7 is launched by the US. Its mission produces 4,316 pictures of the surface of the Moon with six spacecraft cameras. Close-ups of the lunar surface for the first time show the astonishing array of craters and boulders.

August 28 Weather forecasting from space using Nimbus series of meteorological satellites begins.

1965 March Gemini spacecraft succeed NASA's Mercury spaceships with a vehicle twice as big.

July 15 Mariner 4, launched November 24, 1964, flies past Mars to return the first close-up pictures of another planet. The photographs dispose of the long controversy about what looked like Martian canals from Earth. A Moon-like dead planet is seen.

1966 March 1 The first man-made machine to land on another planet is the crash-landing of the Russian Venera 3 on Venus.

August 10 Start of the Lunar Orbiter 1 by NASA, for systematic mapping of the potential landing sites on the Moon, by a probe carrying high resolution cameras in a low orbit.

1967 Jan 27 The Apollo 1 disaster occurs. Due for launching in March, the crew were running tests when an electrical fire caused the deaths of Virgil Grissom, Edward White and Roger Chaffee. The tragedy delays the Apollo Moon program by 19 months.

1967 April 24 Vladimir Komarov, the first Russian cosmonaut to be given a second flight, dies in a crash landing of Soyuz 1. The parachute for braking became tangled.

1969 July 20 Neil Armstrong becomes the first man to set foot on the Moon, when the American spacecraft code-named Eagle lands at Tranquility Base.

1971 Salyut 1, which was the forerunner of the Salyut 7, and *Mir* permanent space stations are pioneered by the Russians.

1975 July 15 The only time when East and West meet in space, with the Apollo-Soyuz link-up and the transfer of the American and Russian crews between each others' spaceships. It is the most complicated count-down in the short history of space flight.

1981 April 12 On the anniversary of Gagarin's first flight, the American space shuttle makes its debut with the Orbiter Columbia taking veteran astronauts John Young and Robert Crippen into space.

1986 January The American space program is grounded for two years with the explosion of space shuttle Challenger.

▷ Ariane, ESA's launch vehicle, separates from its booster rockets after taking off.

Index

Photographic credits:
Cover: Rex Features; cover insert, pages 4-5, 17 and 22-23: Frank Spooner Agency; pages 6 (left and top right), 7, 10-11, 28-29 and 29: NASA; page 6 (bottom): Visnews; pages 8 and 24: The Research House; pages 11, 14-15 and 25: European Space Agency; pages 12, 12-13, 15, 20 and 28: Science Photo Library; page 16: David Baker/Sigma Projects; page 18: Deutsche Press Agentur; page 21: Daily Telegraph/Space Frontiers; pages 22 and 23 (top): Photosource; pages 25 and back cover: British Aerospace; pages 26-27 and 27: Popperfoto: page 31: Aerospatiale.